Rainwater Harvesting

A Sustainable Solution for Water Management

Table of Contents

Chapter 1. Introduction

In this enlightening Special Report, we dive into the realm of Rainwater Harvesting, a sustainable and eco-friendly solution that is revolutionizing water management across the globe. We've strived to make this complex topic approachable and engaging, highlighting the practical applications, benefits, and the potential this concept holds for solving pressing water issues. Whether you're passionately green, a technical enthusiast, a policy-maker, or simply someone interested in learning about sustainable innovations, this report will open your eyes to how each raindrop, when harvested, can contribute to a brighter, more water-secure future. Our easy-to-understand approach will keep you hooked, making you feel like this report is absolutely a must-have piece for your collection. Come, let's enjoy the journey to understand our environment better and explore ways to preserve it one raindrop at a time with 'Rainwater Harvesting: A Sustainable Solution for Water Management.'

Chapter 2. Unveiling the Concept of Rainwater Harvesting

Rainwater harvesting could be coined as the "revival of a lost art" in modern society. It is a technique where we put nature's wisdom and our traditional knowledge into use, blending it with modern technology, to address the contemporary water crisis. With expanding towns and dwindling water resources, the need to collect and store rainwater has re-emerged as an urgent issue.

2.1. Historical Background

Historically, rainwater harvesting is not a new concept or sudden enlightenment. It can be traced back to ancient civilizations including those in the Arabian Peninsula, India, and Rome, where they used these methods to provide supplementary water, primarily for agriculture and later for domestic consumption. They developed sophisticated rainwater harvesting systems by constructing dams, canals, and reservoirs enabling them to extend their agriculture into regions that are now considered arid. The wisdom of rain collecting is an age-old practice we are rediscovered for our current needs.

2.2. Understanding the Concept

Essentially, at its heart, rainwater harvesting is the accumulation and deposition of rainwater for reuse rather than allowing it to run off. It includes the collection, filtration, storage, and use of rainwater. The system can be as simple as rain barrels placed under a roof's downspout to collect water for garden irrigation, or as complex as a complete home system providing the majority of the water used in the household.

2.3. What Do We Harvest?

When we talk about rainwater harvesting, we refer primarily to harvesting atmospheric precipitation, usually on roofs. Other surface areas like parking lots, roads or compounds can also be used, under certain conditions. We intercept, generally speaking, rain. However, depending on the system and purpose, it might also involve collecting surface runoff or even seasonal floodwater.

2.4. Elements of Rainwater Harvesting

The basic elements of a rainwater harvesting system include catchment area (typically the rooftop), gutters and downspouts, leaf screens and roof washers, storage tanks (cisterns), and a delivery system. The size and complexity of these components can vary depending on the use of the harvested rainwater and the integration into an existing water supply system.

A slightly inclined, non-porous rooftop is a good catchment location. Downspouts and gutters transport the rainwater from the catchment location towards the cistern. Leaf screens and roof washers prevent debris and dust from entering the cistern. Then, the water from the cistern can be pumped to the point of use or fed into the main water supply line.

2.5. Storage of Harvested Rainwater

Storage is one of the most critical parts in the process of rainwater harvesting. The type of storage system depends on factors like the volume of rainwater to be stored, the purpose of the water, the space available, and the cost. In settings with ample space and less demand, open ponds, dams, and reservoirs might be used. In other scenarios, where the demand is high and space is constrained, elaborate underground storage tanks and cisterns would be constructed.

In most domestic rainwater harvesting setups, water is usually stored in a tank or barrel. Depending on the availability of space and budget, the tank may be above ground and visible, below ground and out of sight, or positioned in a basement.

2.6. Water Quality Considerations

The quality of harvested rainwater can be influenced by several factors – the cleanliness of the roof and gutters, the volume of bird or animal droppings, atmospheric pollution, and contamination from leaves or debris in the water. The larger the catchment area, the more significant these influences become. Therefore, while rainwater is not typically potable immediately upon collection, it can be purified for drinking purposes through filtration, disinfection techniques like chlorination, or boiling.

2.7. Applications of Rainwater Harvesting

Rainwater can serve a variety of non-potable needs in the household, including flushing toilets, washing clothes, watering the garden, or washing cars, thereby significantly reducing the demand on conventional water supplies. Moreover, in farming and agriculture, the harvested water can be used for irrigation, livestock, and general farming needs, meaning massive cost savings and eco-friendly farming practices.

Industry too can benefit immensely. Many factories use water as a coolant, and harvested rainwater, post basic treatment, could meet this large-scale requirement, making industries self-reliant for their water needs while conserving water resources.

In this era of advancing technology and environmental

consciousness, it is indeed heartening to see the revival of this age-old wisdom. Rainwater harvesting is a sustainable, environmentally friendly, and economically sound method of managing our water resources adaptively, assuring a water-secure future. The concept is simple, but the implications and impact are profound, as every drop of water saved is a step toward a sustainable future.

Chapter 3. History and Evolution of Rainwater Harvesting

Rainwater harvesting, as a concept, is far from new. Its roots sink deeply into humanity's early history, evolving over time with cultural growth and technological advancement. With the marriage of necessity and ingenuity, early civilizations discovered that water—an essential resource for sustaining life—could be harnessed from the sky.

3.1. Ancient Civilizations and the Birth of Rainwater Harvesting

Our narrative begins with ancient civilizations, from around 3000 BC, when the Indus Valley Civilization in present-day Pakistan and northwest India implemented one of the earliest known rainwater harvesting systems. Here, towns like Dholavira built impressive citywide water conservation systems, featuring reservoirs fed by a network of channels and drains to capture monsoon rains.

A jump across the globe takes us to the Island of Crete, where the famous palace of Knossos, the hub of the Minoan civilization (2000-1600 BC), utilized large pottery cisterns buried underground for domestic rainwater storage. A similar practice was adopted by the Roman Empire, spreading across Europe and the Middle East.

In South America, the Nazca culture of Peru (1 AD to 700 AD) deployed underground 'puquios' systems, which used the flow of water to bring torrential rainwater from the Andes to dry lowlands. Meanwhile, their contemporaries, the Mayans in Mexico and Central America, used 'chultuns'—lime-plastered underground storage—for collecting rainwater, hinting at a universal recognition of harvesting rain among these civilizations.

3.2. Middle Ages to Colonial Period: Thriving Systems and Challenges

As societies progressed, innovative techniques for rainwater harvesting emerged. In the Middle Ages, farmers across Europe built ridge-and-furrow fields which, in addition to aiding the growth of crops, effectively gathered and stored rainwater. The Ancient Egyptians and later the Byzantine Empire pioneered water collection from rooftops and roads, a precursor to modern urban rainwater harvesting.

Despite these advancements, the gathering momentum of rainwater harvesting stuttered during the Colonial period. As colonizers introduced piped water systems that diverted water from rivers and lakes, the reliance on rainwater harvesting diminished in many regions. Still, indigenous populations and remote communities clung to their traditional methods and knowledge as part of their cultural identity.

3.3. Industrial Age to Early 20th Century: Neglect and Rediscovery

By the dawn of the Industrial Age, largely due to the increased complexity of water and sanitation infrastructure, rainwater harvesting was completely overshadowed in developed nations. The principal focus shifted towards centralized supply systems that offered seemingly endless volumes of water, paid little attention to resource depletion, and disregarded the value or potential of harnessed rainfall.

Ironically, this period also marks the scientific recognition of the global hydrological cycle, which revealed nature's own method of desalinating, purifying, and evenly distributing water—processes embodied by rainwater harvesting.

It wasn't until the mid-20th century, driven by a need for sustainable solutions in water-scarce areas and heightened awareness of water conservation, that rainwater harvesting was recognized anew. Various experiments and small-scale implementations began cropping up, marking a resurgence of this age-old wisdom.

3.4. Late 20th Century to Present: A Renaissance and Evolution

In the last few decades, as environmental awareness has grown, harvesting rainfall has seen an upsurge in popularity and innovation. Particularly in arid and semi-arid regions, the practices have evolved and been enhanced using modern technology. Additionally, concerns regarding climate change and its impact on water scarcity have propelled rainwater harvesting into the discourse of sustainable solutions for water management.

Modern rainwater harvesting systems, from rooftop collection installations to large-scale public systems, incorporate advanced filtration, storage, and distribution technology, making harvested water suitable for various uses—from irrigation and cleaning to potable water supply, with appropriate treatment.

Even in urban environments—with landscapes far separated from their natural state—a new generation of municipal policies and green building trends promote rainwater harvesting. In this context, it's used to reduce stormwater runoff, supplement potable water supplies, and conserve energy otherwise used for water treatment and transportation.

The history of rainwater harvesting presents us with a rich tapestry of resilience, adaptation, neglect, and rejuvenation. It's the tale of an ever-relevant technique—to harness nature's bounty, value every drop, and enlist rain as a partner in the pursuit of water security, proving that each storm is indeed a silver lining for water management. Human history, in this aspect, flows with the fluidity of water itself, from the epochs of the past into the promise of tomorrow.

Chapter 4. The Science Behind Harvesting Rainwater

In the context of a rapidly changing global milieu, the advent and adoption of rainwater harvesting can be compared to a refreshing oasis within the desert of water scarcity. It's crucial to have a sound understanding of the science behind this potentially transformative technology to fully comprehend its potential and applications.

4.1. How Does It Work?

Rainwater harvesting is a relatively simple concept at its core. It involves three basic steps: collect, filter, and store. Rain that falls on the rooftop of a building or any other catchment is directed, either through natural slopes or installed gutter systems, into a filtering system before being stored in tanks or infiltrated into the soil for future use.

The effectiveness of rainwater harvesting systems depends on several factors. These include the size of the catchment area, the number of rainfall events, rainfall intensity, climatic conditions, and water demand. Determining the size of the storage tank for a given water demand requires knowledge of the region's rainfall pattern and the efficiency of the system itself. One square meter of roof area can collect approximately 0.85 cubic meters of water during a year with 1000 mm of rainfall.

4.2. Quality Aspects of Harvested Rainwater

Rainwater is generally clean. However, it can deteriorally in quality when it comes into contact with unclean rooftops, birds' droppings, dead leaves, dust, and particulates in the air. The first wash of water from a rain event that washes down the pollutants from the roof is typically not collected or is diverted to ensure good quality water is captured.

Rainwater collection systems also include pre-treatment processes, such as filtration and disinfection, to improve the quality of captured water before it's stored or used. Once the harvested water is stored, it undergoes natural purification processes, including sedimentation and biological activity at the base of the storage tank, which help to improve overall water quality.

4.3. Architectural Integration

The catchment area is one of the most critical elements in rainwater harvesting. In urban contexts, rooftops are the most common catchment surfaces. The larger the surface area, the more water can be captured. A flat or gently sloping roof made up of non-toxic, smooth material such as corrugated iron or tiles is best suited for rainwater harvesting, as they allow maximum rainwater capture and quick run-off, reducing chances of contamination.

Integration with building infrastructure typically involves installing gutters and downpipes to direct rainwater into the storage system. A first flush diverter can be part of this, allowing the initial dirty flush of rainwater to be diverted away from the storage system.

4.4. Rainwater Storage Systems

Once the rainwater is collected and filtered, it is stored for future use. Storage systems can range from simple rain barrels to more complex underground cisterns. The choice of storage container will depend on the local climate, the intended use of the rainwater, and the available budget.

In regions with high evaporation rates, it might be more appropriate to store harvested rainwater in underground tanks to reduce water loss. Conversely, in colder climates prone to freezing, above-ground storage may be more suitable. It is also essential to secure storage tanks to prevent them from becoming habitats for mosquitoes or other pests.

The storage tank's size is key to guarantee a continuous supply, particularly during non-rainy periods. A simple balance can be struck between meeting the maximum possible demand and the cost of the tank by using rainfall data.

4.5. Employing Harvested Rainwater

Once stored, harvested rainwater can be used for various purposes, including garden irrigation, toilet flushing, washing clothes, topping up swimming pools, and even drinking if purified adequately. Employing harvested water for non-potable uses not only provides a vital alternative water source but drastically reduces dependency on treated water for such uses, saving both water and energy.

4.6. Challenges and Sustainability Aspects

While rainwater harvesting is a promising solution to water scarcity, it faces a few challenges. These include fulfilling water needs during prolonged periods of no rainfall, maintaining the quality of stored rainwater, and legal restrictions in some regions.

Sustainability is an integral aspect of rainwater harvesting systems, beneficial in several ways - reduction in stormwater runoff causing flood mitigation, elevation of groundwater levels due to infiltration systems, and actively contributing to energy savings, as the process of filtering and treating rainwater is less intensive compared to conventional water treatment methods.

In conclusion, the science behind rainwater harvesting is an intricate blend of simple catchment techniques, sophisticated filtration processes, and strategic storage methodologies. Embedded within it, we find a sincere endeavor towards sustainable water management.

Chapter 5. Global Water Crisis and the Role of Rainwater Harvesting

Every drop of water counts, especially in a world where water scarcity is a stark reality. Today, approximately 2.2 billion people lack access to safely managed drinking water services, as reported by the United Nations (UN). Global water scarcity is fast becoming one of humanity's most pressing concerns, as climatic variability and human pressure intensify its impact on every continent.

However, not all hope is lost. Amid the troubling statistics, one solution stands out as both practical and sustainable, with the potential to revolutionize how we perceive and manage water in the 21st century — rainwater harvesting (RWH).

5.1. The Escalating Global Water Crisis

Water scarcity globally has become a crisis due to the growing disparity between water demand and availability. The UN predicts that by 2025, two-thirds of the world population could be under stress conditions caused by water scarcity, while half of them will be living in water-stressed areas.

Factors leading to the crisis are manifold: population growth, increased urbanization, agricultural expansion, industrial growth, and climate change are some of the key contributors. The gap between the supply and demand for water continues to widen, leading to an alarming reality where some regions are tremendously water-stressed, and others are water-rich.

The World Health Organization (WHO) reports that one-third of all schools worldwide lack access to basic water and sanitation services, affecting education and health outcomes dramatically. Furthermore, these conditions increase the risk of waterborne diseases and contribute to cyclical poverty.

With surface groundwater levels receding worldwide, the prospect of finding new freshwater sources is slim. Hence, innovative approaches for sustainable water management are likely to play a critical role in combating the global water crisis.

5.2. Rainwater Harvesting: An Antidote to the Water Crisis?

Enter: Rainwater Harvesting. Simply put, RWH is the collection, filtration, storage (and in some cases treatment) of rainwater for various purposes such as irrigation, household use, or groundwater recharge, which can be a game changer in managing the looming water crisis.

Rainwater is a valuable resource that, for the longest time, has been hugely overlooked. The beauty of rainwater harvesting lies in its simplicity — these systems can range from simple rain barrels beneath a home's downspout, to more extensive underground cisterns that collect runoff from building roofs or other impervious surfaces.

5.3. Utilizing and Maximizing Rainwater

Worldwide, rainwater harvesting is proving to be a significant tool in the fight against water scarcity. People have begun to realize that managing water doesn't always mean finding new resources, but making the most of what's readily, and often freely available.

However, for RWH to gain broader acceptance, public awareness, policy support, technical know-how, and financial resources need to be invested to develop resilient water systems, primarily due to the misconstrued notion that harvested rainwater is inferior to other sources.

Yet, when properly collected and treated, rainwater can meet drinking water quality standards outlined by the WHO. This practice not only reduces our dependence on ground and surface water but also mitigates the adverse effects of stormwater runoff.

Rainwater harvesting carries a myriad of benefits: it decentralizes water supply, reduces water bills, aids in drought mitigation, lowers demand on municipal systems, and contributes to battling climate change by reducing carbon emissions associated with water delivery.

5.4. Policy Push and Technological Innovations

The global community has been acknowledging these facts, as we see more policies that incentivize RWH across various regions. In Bermuda and the U.S. Virgin Islands, for example, every new house is legally required to include a rainwater harvesting system.

Likewise, technological advancements are making it easier to collect and store rainwater. Innovations in filtration systems have improved the quality of harvested water and reduced maintenance costs. Applications of AI and IoT in these systems have also enhanced efficiency and ease of use, making rainwater harvesting more accessible than ever.

Innovative designs and community participation, especially in developing nations, have made way for low-cost solutions that can serve entire communities. Schools and hospitals in these areas have become pioneers, managing their water supply and influencing their local communities.

5.5. Realization: The Drop Counts

Rain-water harvesting isn't just a solution to global water scarcity; it's a call to each individual, each community to understand the value of each drop. It also reinforces the quintessential principle that our survival is intertwined: what we do to nature, ultimately we do to ourselves.

To conclude, the escalating global water crisis ties directly with the ethical and ecological need to encourage and adopt sustainable water management techniques like rainwater harvesting. The role of rainwater harvesting in the global water crisis may not be a silver bullet solution to all our water woes, however, it has significant potential to put us on a path towards a more sustainable and water-secure future.

Chapter 6. Practical Techniques for Rainwater Collection and Storage

Rainwater harvesting is not a nascent concept. It has been practiced for centuries in diverse parts of the world, each employing distinctive yet highly ingenious processes. As the world grapples with water scarcity, a renewed focus has been placed on these traditional wisdoms, coupled with modern technologies, to optimize rainwater capture and storage.

The most effective methods for the collection and storage of rainwater can be classified into two major categories: surface runoff harvesting and rooftop rainwater harvesting. Of the two, the latter boasts the most widespread utilization due to its relative simplicity and efficiency.

6.1. Surface Runoff Harvesting Techniques

Surface runoff harvesting essentially involves the collection of water that moves over the earth's surface during and after a period of rain. This method is particularly efficacious in hilly or sloping regions where the runoff's flow velocity aids in collection.

A popular technique is the construction of check dams, these structures act like speed-breakers, reducing the kinetic energy of running water, and enabling useful water pooling for further use.

In flat and semi-arid areas, dug-out ponds, also known as 'farm ponds,' can be implemented. Runoff water can be guided into these excavations with the help of small channels. The concept is to allow for maximum water percolation, which recharges the groundwater tables.

For urban settings, permeable pavements offer a viable solution. These advanced materials allow rainwater to percolate into the subsoil, preventing surface waterlogging and replenishing underground water reserves.

6.2. Rooftop Rainwater Harvesting Techniques

Although surface runoff harvesting techniques hold significant potential, rooftop rainwater harvesting remains the most practiced process, particularly for urban residential and industrial settings. This system is simple, cost-effective, and yields high-quality water, making it suitable for various end uses.

A standard rooftop harvesting system involves several key components:

- Catchment: The roof of a building serves as the catchment area. The smoother the surface, the higher the amount and quality of collected water.

- Conveyance system: Gutters and downspouts constitute the conveyance mechanisms. They channel the water from the catchment to the storage, ensuring minimal leakages and contamination.

- First-flush: It is a valve system designed to divert the initial flow of water which often carries contaminants and debris from the roof surface.

- Filter: Before entering the storage, water passes through a filtration system that removes any residual impurities.

- Storage tank: Collected water is stored in tanks, which can vary significantly in size and material. They should be dark and sealed to prevent algal growth and insect infestation.

- Recharge structure: If the storage tank overflows, the system should include a mechanism to divert this excess water into a recharge pit. This helps in reducing waterlogging while aiding in groundwater replenishment.

6.3. Enhancements in Rainwater Harvesting Techniques

While the principles of rainwater harvesting have remained the same, technological advancements have made these systems more efficient, easy-to-maintain, and user-friendly. Automated rainwater harvesting systems are now available that offer advanced filtering options, reduced manual intervention, and optimal design efficiencies.

Moreover, smart rainwater tanks can communicate with weather forecasting systems to anticipate rainfall and accordingly, adjust their holding levels. They ensure storage capacity is maximized without the risk of overflow.

In addition, other cutting-edge technologies, like polyethylene tanks, offer benefits like easy installation, low maintenance, and high durability, thus adding to the overall efficiency of the rainwater harvesting system.

Rainwater harvesting does not only offer practical benefits but provides numerous ecological advantages as well. Employing the aforesaid techniques can conserve water, reduce dependence on municipal supplies, lessen the impact of droughts, and ensure a sustainable and secure water future. Therefore, the implication and understanding of these techniques, whether you live in an urban condo or a sprawling farm, holds significance for all.

Chapter 7. Designing Effective Rainwater Harvesting Systems for Urban and Rural Settings

Rainwater Harvesting Systems (RHS) vary considerably in complexity, depending on factors such as the local climate, the intended use of the water, and available space. They can range from a simple rain barrel at the bottom of a downspout to more comprehensive systems that can provide water for a whole house. Our aim in this section is to help you understand the essential components of a rainwater harvesting system and to explain how they are combined to create systems suited to different settings. Whether your circumstances are rural or urban, and whether the intended use is for irrigation, indoor use or for replenishing groundwater, there are strategies and designs available to you. To make this a practical guide, we'll delve into details, share diagrams and outline best practices. Let's embark on this journey to design effective rainwater harvesting systems.

=== Designing Simple RHS for Beginners

A simple RHS can easily be installed in your home regardless of whether you live in an urban dwelling or on a rural property. For this type of system, the essential components are a catchment surface (typically a roof), a method of conveyance (such as gutters and downspouts), and a storage unit (such as a rain barrel or cistern).

The catchment surface should be relatively smooth and impervious to ensure optimal water collection. For most homes, the roof is the most accessible high surface area catchment surface. Taking into consideration the slope of the roof, roofing material and local climate will allow for a more nuanced set up for rain collection.

The conveyance system facilitates the movement of rainwater from the catchment surface to the storage unit. For most homes, this involves using existing gutters and downspouts. However, the conveyance system may require some tweaking to ensure that it directs water effectively into your storage unit.

The choice of a storage unit is determined by the amount of water you expect to collect and use. For small-scale RHS, a rain barrel with a capacity of 150-200 liters will suffice. It's usually placed at the bottom of the downspout and has a spout or pump for withdrawing water. A lid is necessary to prevent the breeding of mosquitos.

A simple urban rainwater harvesting system

```
image::simpleRHS.png[A simple urban rainwater harvesting
system]
```

The above image provides an overview of a simple RHS typically designed for an urban setup. A similar design can also be applied to rural settings with minor adjustments.

=== Expanding to More Complex RHS

For those who want to harvest rainwater on a larger scale or utilize it for more applications (like indoor use or groundwater recharge), a more complex system may be required. Although more intricate, the underlying structure of these systems remains consistent with the simpler models, including the need for a catchment surface, conveyance, and storage. However, additional components such as filters, first-flush diverters, pumps, and treatment systems can elevate the capacities of these systems providing more extensive use of the captured rainwater.

Expanding on design concepts

```
image::complexRHS.png[An integrated rainwater harvesting
system]
```

The diagram above expands on the design of basic RHS, incorporating filtering, a first-flush diverter, a pumping mechanism, and a treatment system to illustrate a more complex system typically used for indoor purposes and at large properties.

=== Relating Design to Intended Use

The design components of an RHS need to be thoughtfully put together not only based on space, budget and met climatic conditions, but also on the intended end-use of the collected rainwater.

For potable use, besides all these components, an appropriate treatment system to purify the water is required.

Here are some design recommendations based on the intended use of rainwater.

Table 1. End-use and Corresponding Design

End-use	Design Requirements
Irrigation	Rain Barrel with a basic filter
Non-potable indoor use	Cistern, First Flush Diverter, Basic Filter, Pump
Potable use	Cistern, First Flush Diverter, Advanced Filter, Pump, Adequate Treatment System

Links between the intended use and design requirements provide a practical guide for setting up your own RHS.

=== Regional and Geographical Considerations

The design of an RHS should also take into consideration the climate and geography of the location. If you live in a region with well-defined wet and dry seasons, the size of storage units should be large enough to capture water in the rainy seasons and slowly utilize it in drier periods. For colder regions, the design of RHS should account for any issues relating to freezing.

When it comes to geographical considerations, in urban settings, it can be difficult to construct large cistern systems due to space constraints. Consider the use of underground cisterns and the maximization of vertical space in such cases. In rural settings, the luxurious availability of space often allows for larger catchment surfaces and larger storage volumes.

In conclusion, designing effective rainwater harvesting systems requires an in-depth understanding of the fundamental components, thoughtful consideration of their integration, and a careful alignment with local conditions and end-use expectations. By taking these aspects into account, we can create systems that provide a sustainable water source while helping to alleviate the strain on traditional water sources. Remember, every drop counts!

Chapter 8. Analyzing the Cost-benefit Relationship of Rainwater Harvesting

When evaluating the merit of rainwater harvesting, one of the fundamental aspects to consider is the cost-benefit relationship. This involves a detailed analysis of upfront investments needed, operational costs, and the considerable benefits accrued over time, both tangible and intangible.

8.1. The Financial Dimension: Initial Investment and Operational Costs

Understanding the cost aspect of rainwater harvesting requires us to look at certain key components. These include the design and installation expenses, purchasing costs for tank, pipes, roof catchment area, and water treatment setup, and the recurring operation and maintenance costs.

Firstly, the design and installation charges vary widely based on local labor cost, the expertise required, and the specifics of the installation site. It usually involves site assessment, rainwater catchment and storage design, system installation, and quality control checks.

Tank size is another major determinant of the initial costs. With various sizes available, it's critical to balance between the upfront investment and future utility. On average, the cost of a rainwater tank varies between $0.50 to $2.00 per gallon of water it can store.

Pipes, gutters, and other components add to the initial investment. Costs can range from $2 to $8 per linear foot for gutters and between $0.50 to $2.00 per linear foot for pipes.

Treating the collected rainwater for consumption (if desired) requires an additional setup. This can include filters and disinfecting systems like UV or chlorine injection, typically ranging between $100 to $1000 based on system sophistication.

Furthermore, operational costs encompass routine maintenance, electricity, and scheduled treatment of water (if applicable).

It's important to note, however, these costs and estimates may fluctuate based on a variety of factors - geographical location, climate, material costs, and the desired sophistication of the setup.

8.2. Harvesting the Benefits: Quantifiable and Beyond

Shift your perspective to the benefits reaped from rainwater harvesting, and you can see why it's a sustainable solution worth the investment.

The most direct benefit is a significant reduction in your water bills. By utilizing captured rainwater for non-potable uses such as irrigation, laundry, toilets, and cleaning, dependency on the municipal supply diminishes considerably. In many jurisdictions, fee rebates are available for those investing in harvesting systems, aiding in offsetting the setup costs.

Not only does rainwater harvesting reduce demand on communal water supplies, but it also minimizes impact on local watersheds and reduces stormwater runoff, an often-overlooked benefit. It helps prevent soil erosion, reduces flooding, and ultimately contributes to healthier rivers and streams.

Another quantifiable long-term benefit is the resilience provided during droughts or water restrictions. By ensuring a private source of water, rainwater harvesting can be particularly beneficial in water-scarce regions.

In addition, using rainwater for garden irrigation improves the health of plants. It's often naturally soft, devoid of the hardness minerals and chlorine commonly present in municipal water, making it a more suitable watering solution.

Looking beyond monetary benefits, the ecological cushioning rainwater harvesting provides is invaluable. It fosters a culture of conservation, assists in replenishing groundwater, and bolsters your green profile.

8.3. Cost-benefit Analysis: Seeking the Break-even Point

Given the complexity of the costs and benefits associated with rainwater harvesting, a simple return on investment may not suffice to capture its true value. To determine the break-even point for a rainwater harvesting system, including the tangible and intangible benefits into the calculation is vital.

While the overall equation may change based on particular circumstances, the following is a simplistic representation:

The break-even point (in years) = (Upfront cost + Annual operational cost / Annual water bill savings + Value of environmental benefits)

Despite initial upfront investment, the benefits – reduced water bills, resilience during drought, ecological advantages – in the long run make the investment worthwhile.

When considering the cost-benefit analysis of rainwater harvesting, it's vital not to overlook the intangible benefits that don't come with a quantifiable value. By redefining our relationship with water, rainwater harvesting encourages environmental stewardship, stimulates a more empowering attitude towards consumption, and ultimately promotes water security in your community.

Rainwater harvesting hinges on the belief that every drop counts. While the initial investment may seem substantial, the long-term benefits and contribution to global water security make it a solution that has no substitute. Its cost-effectiveness renews itself every time it rains, garnering benefits for individuals, communities, and ecosystems alike. Let's make every raindrop matter, and see it for the precious resource it truly is.

Chapter 9. Legislation, Policies, and Incentives Around Rainwater Harvesting

As rainwater harvesting increasingly gains global recognition for its pivotal role in alleviating water scarcity and promoting sustainability, it is imperative to cast a light on the legislation, policies, and incentives that forge its successful implementation.

Several governments, both national and local, around the world have been progressively recognizing the potential environmental and economic benefits that rainwater harvesting systems can offer. Incorporating these systems into their water management strategies requires shifting legislative structures, creating supportive policies, and providing financial incentives to encourage individuals and businesses to adopt rainwater harvesting.

9.1. Global Legislations on Rainwater Harvesting

Although there is no universal legislation governing rainwater harvesting, numerous countries have set up their frameworks integrating the practice.

For instance, Australia stands at the forefront, particularly the city of Melbourne, which tackled its drought issues by mandating rainwater harvesting in all new properties since 2004. Besides, its national program, "Water Efficiency Labelling and Standards (WELS)" encourages the efficient use of water and stimulates innovation in water-saving technologies.

In Germany, Berlin's Rainwater Management Concept promotes the use of rainwater for non-potable services, while offering stormwater fee discounts to properties installing rainwater harvesting systems.

In India, the Central Ground Water Authority issued an advisory mandating all institutional buildings, residential societies, and individual households to install rainwater harvesting structures.

Across these diverse legislative efforts worldwide, there emerges a common theme: the recognition that rainwater harvesting is key to sustainable water management.

9.2. Policies Encouraging Rainwater Harvesting

Policy provisions craft the practical landscape for rainwater harvesting uptake. Policies for rainwater harvesting broadly fall into two categories: mandatory requirements and guidelines.

Mandatory requirements enforce rainwater harvesting as essential for new or certain categories of building development. For example, Tokyo mandates all new large buildings to install rainwater harvesting Systems in its metropolitan waterworks' law.

On the other hand, guidelines provide a mapped-out direction for rainwater harvesting but lack enforceable mandates. The UK's 'Building Regulations: Guidance Document G', for instance, offers succinct guidelines on water efficiency, including rainwater harvesting.

9.3. Financial Incentives for Rainwater Harvesting

Governments worldwide have been acknowledging the financial

constraints of rainwater harvesting installations by providing ways to alleviate these costs.

Financial incentives offered include grants, tax incentives, loans, subsidies, and stormwater fee reductions. These can be exceptionally compelling; for instance, the city of Portland, USA, offers financial assistance for rain gardens or other on-site stormwater management systems, drastically reducing installation costs.

In Barbados, citizens can claim 100% of the expenses of purchasing and installing a rainwater harvesting system from their income taxes, under the 'Water Conservation Measures Relating to Taxation Act'.

These financial incentives have a significant influence over public decision about installing a rainwater harvesting system.

9.4. Overcoming Legislative and Policy Challenges

Despite advances in legislation and policy for rainwater harvesting, challenges persist. These derive predominantly from traditional water management practices and diverse perceptions on rainwater harvesting. Moreover, the legal framework becomes complex because water management falls into local, regional and national jurisdiction.

An effective and comprehensive legislation-policy package must focus on striking a balance between encouragement through incentives, and enforcement through laws and regulations. They must also factor in local geographical and climatic conditions, water needs, and socio-economic status.

In conclusion, all stakeholders, including policy makers, water and urban planners, and citizens, play a part in promoting rainwater harvesting. Progressive policies, effective legislations, and attractive incentives form the backbone of successful adoption of rainwater harvesting systems globally.

This comparative examination of legislation, policies, and incentives serves as a stepping stone to identifying best practices. It reveals the crucial role that socio-political measures play in enabling or inhibiting the implementation and uptake of rainwater harvesting. Let this evidence guide nations yet to embark on this route, with lessons and inspiration for nurturing a sustainable, more water-secure future.

Chapter 10. Impact of Rainwater Harvesting on Ecosystems and Biodiversity

Rainwater harvesting is not just about utilizing an abundant natural resource; it also has profound implications for the health and wellbeing of our ecosystems and biodiversity. When implemented effectively, this method of water management can contribute significantly to the conservation and enhancement of the environment, promoting biodiversity and contributing to a healthier, more resilient ecosystem.

10.1. The Role of Rainwater Harvesting in Ecosystem Conservation

Ecosystems around the world are under increasing stress because of anthropogenic factors such as deforestation, overexploitation of resources, and climate change. However, rainwater harvesting offers a potential solution to these challenges. By collecting and storing rainwater for use during periods of low rainfall or drought, it alleviates the pressure on water sources that would otherwise be overused, allowing ecosystems to recuperate and thrive.

Moreover, the utilization of harvested rainwater ensures a local source of water that is adaptive to the specific ecosystem's needs. This proximity plays a critical role in maintaining a balance in the water cycle, a pivotal mechanism in ecosystem function.

10.2. The Positive Impact on Soil Health

Soil is one of the most important components of ecosystems and biodiversity, as it houses numerous microorganisms and functions as a critical resource for land-based life forms. When rainwater is harvested and used efficiently, it reduces soil erosion and sedimentation that may be resulted from storm runoff, thus preserving valuable topsoil. This practice also contributes to increase soil moisture levels, which is beneficial for plant life and microbial communities in the soil, in turn supporting other species in the food web.

Additionally, as rainwater is naturally soft, it doesn't contain minerals such as calcium and magnesium that hard water does. When used for irrigation, it decreases the risk of soil salinization, which can become a major issue with prolonged use of groundwater or certain surface water.

10.3. Enhancing Biodiversity through Rainwater Harvesting

Biodiversity, the variety and variability of life on Earth, is at the heart of ecosystem function. Rainwater harvesting can support biodiversity directly and indirectly through a number of ways.

Firstly, it creates new habitats for wildlife. Constructed facilities for rainwater collection, such as rain gardens or ponds, can double up as habitats for a variety of fauna and flora.

Secondly, the water collected can serve as a vital resource for wildlife, especially in urban environments where natural water sources are scarce. This additional water source helps support bird populations, insects like bees and butterflies which are essential for pollination, and other wildlife within the ecosystem.

The indirect benefits are just as important. As rainwater harvesting supports healthier soils and plants, it can also lead to more diverse plant communities. This promotes a diversity of insects, birds, and other fauna, fostering a more vibrant ecosystem.

10.4. Rainwater Harvesting and Climate Change Mitigation

One aspect of ecosystem preservation that's particularly important in our current era is climate change mitigation. Effective rainwater harvesting aids in reducing the carbon footprint, as the water collected is naturally dechlorinated and involves no energy-intensive purification processes which are common in municipal water production.

Furthermore, the vegetation supported by rainwater harvesting contributes to carbon sequestration – plants absorb CO_2, a key greenhouse gas, and convert it into oxygen, helping to slow the rate of global warming.

10.5. Conclusion: A Cycle of Enrichment

In the context of increasing environmental degradation and climatic uncertainty, rainwater harvesting presents a symbiotic solution that benefits humanity as well as the ecosystems we inhabit. From replenishing the soils that grow our food to supporting the biodiversity that maintains a balanced and resilient ecosystem, every raindrop harvested is a step towards a healthier planet.

Nonetheless, while this sustainable practice holds much potential, it is not a standalone tool. Rainwater harvesting must be integrated into broader sustainable water management and land use strategies, combined with measures such as water conservation, pollution prevention, and forest regeneration. Only through such multi-pronged approaches can we preserve the ecosystems upon which all life depends.

Understanding and exploiting the benefits that rainwater harvesting brings to the ecosystem require knowledge, effort, and investment, but every drop of water saved and every species protected is a testament to the potency of sustainable living. Rainwater Harvesting is just one gear in the complex mechanics of environmental stewardship, nevertheless, it's a vital one that shifts us closer to a more sustainable and resilient future.

Chapter 11. Sustainability and Future Prospects of Rainwater Harvesting

Although rainwater harvesting is a concept steeped in antiquity, its relevance in the face of modern global challenges such as water scarcity and climate change has earned it newfound importance. As we consider the sustainability and future prospects of rainwater harvesting, it is crucial to address these contemporary contexts.

11.1. Defining Sustainability in Rainwater Harvesting

Sustainability might seem like an overused buzzword but it has significant implications for rainwater harvesting. The Brundtland Commission defined sustainable development as "development that meets the needs of the present without compromising the ability of future generations to meet their own needs". In the context of rainwater harvesting, this means generating and sustaining a reliable and safe water source, while adhering to environmental constraints and adapting to changing climatic realities.

Rainwater harvesting makes notable strides towards sustainability. It's a decentralized system that empowers local communities and reduces dependency on centralized water utilities. Collecting water where it falls lowers the need for transportation, reducing energy usage and associated carbon emissions. The harvested rainwater can recharge groundwater aquifers, maintaining their levels and preventing soil subsidence.

11.2. Assessing the Future Prospects of Rainwater Harvesting

Looking ahead, the potential of rainwater harvesting goes far beyond mere water collection. A judicious use of this resource in urban, suburban and rural areas can be a key element in managing climate change and creating sustainable water infrastructures.

Water scarcity is forecasted to intensify, due in part to increasing global temperatures and erratic precipitation patterns. Rainwater harvesting can play a crucial role in supplementing traditional water sources and potentially preventing conflicts over water access. Rainwater is a renewable resource, replenishing naturally during each rainfall event providing individuals and communities with a level of resilience and security against climate change-induced water scarcity. Moreover, by reducing stormwater runoff, it can also minimize urban flooding and the pollution of water bodies.

11.3. The Role of Technology and Innovation

Technological advancements are expected to drive growth and efficiency in rainwater harvesting. Smart technologies can optimize the timing and amount of water collected, reducing waste and ensuring water quality. Similarly, nanotechnology could revolutionize water purification, making the collected rainwater even safer to use.

Further innovations in building design and urban planning incorporating rainwater harvesting could normalize this practice. For example, green buildings and blue-green cities, where natural systems are incorporated into urban infrastructure, may feature rainwater harvesting as a central component. Such applications are promising for institutional, commercial, and residential sectors.

11.4. Policy Implications and Regulatory Frameworks

The future of rainwater harvesting is also linked to policy decisions. Governments can incentivize rainwater harvesting through rebates and subsidies or legislate its inclusion in new developments. Moreover, an integrated approach to water management, where rainwater harvesting is recognized as part of the solution along with traditional water management, can support water security goals.

However, such policies should also consider local realities such as rainfall patterns, geographic characteristics and socio-economic factors. This underscores the need for context-driven, participatory policy-making involving local communities.

11.4.1. Addressing the Bottlenecks

While the future prospects seem promising, several barriers impede the mainstream adoption of rainwater harvesting. Misconceptions about the safety and quality of harvested rainwater, underdeveloped regulatory frameworks, and scarce public awareness are a few common challenges. Efforts must be made to educate the public, foster cultural acceptance, refine regulations, and provide technical support.

11.5. Rainwater Harvesting: Towards a Sustainable Future

As we aspire towards a sustainable water-secure future, rainwater harvesting shows immense promise. By harnessing this age-old practice through technology and innovation, integrating it into our policy and urban design, and addressing the existing barriers, we may evolve a profound, eco-friendly culture of water management. Each raindrop we collect could act as a step towards sustainable development, echoing loudly our commitment to protect the one planet we call home.

Adopting rainwater harvesting is a journey that offers vivid landscapes of learning and profound insights into our own resilience. It heralds a future where rivers are seen not as pipelines running with tap water but as natural, life-giving systems. It rekindles a bond with nature and a respect for the intrinsic value of water. Far beyond a mere technical solution, rainwater harvesting can become a central element of a holistic, sustainable, and respectful relationship with our environment.